Our Animal World

Where Animals Live

by Emily C. Dawson

Amicus Readers are published by Amicus
P.O. Box 1329, Mankato, Minnesota 56002

Copyright © 2011 Amicus. International copyright reserved in all countries.
No part of this book may be reproduced in any form without written permission
from the publisher.

Printed in the United States of America at Corporate Graphics,
North Mankato, Minnesota.

Library of Congress Cataloging-in-Publication Data
Dawson, Emily C.
  Where animals live / by Emily C. Dawson.
     p. cm. – (Amicus readers. Our animal world)
  Includes index.
  Summary: "Describes different continents where animals live and how they live where they can find food. Includes comprehension activity"–Provided by publisher.
  ISBN 978-1-60753-015-2 (library binding)
 1. Animals–Food–Juvenile literature. 2. Zoogeography–Juvenile literature. I. Title.
  QL756.5.D39 2011
  591.9–dc22
                              2010007464

Series Editor   Rebecca Glaser
Series Designer   Kia Adams
Photo Researcher   Heather Dreisbach

Photo Credits
Digital Stock, 6, 8, 20 (m), 21 (b), 22 (tm, br); Jeff Foott/Getty Images, 16, 20 (t), 22 (tl); JH Pete Carmichael/Getty Images, 12–13, 21 (m), 22 (bl); Juniors Bildarchiv/Alamy, 1; Mark Kostich/iStockphoto, cover; Oksana Perkins/iStockphoto, 4–5; Scott Hunt/iStockphoto, 18–19; Tom Ulrich/Getty Images, 14, 20 (b), 22 (bm); worldswildlifewonders/Shutterstock, 10, 21 (t), 22 (tr)

1224
42010

10 9 8 7 6 5 4 3 2 1

Table of Contents

Where Animals Live	6
Picture Glossary	20
What Do You Remember?	22
Ideas for Parents and Teachers	23
Index and Web Sites	24

Wild animals live all around the world. They live where they can find food.

Zebras live in Africa.
Zebras eat short grasses.

Cape buffalo live in Africa, too. They eat tall grasses. They live near water.

Spider monkeys live in South America. They eat fruits and nuts from rain forest trees.

Tree frogs live in South America, too. They eat insects and spiders.

Rattlesnakes live in North America. They eat mice, rats, and rabbits.

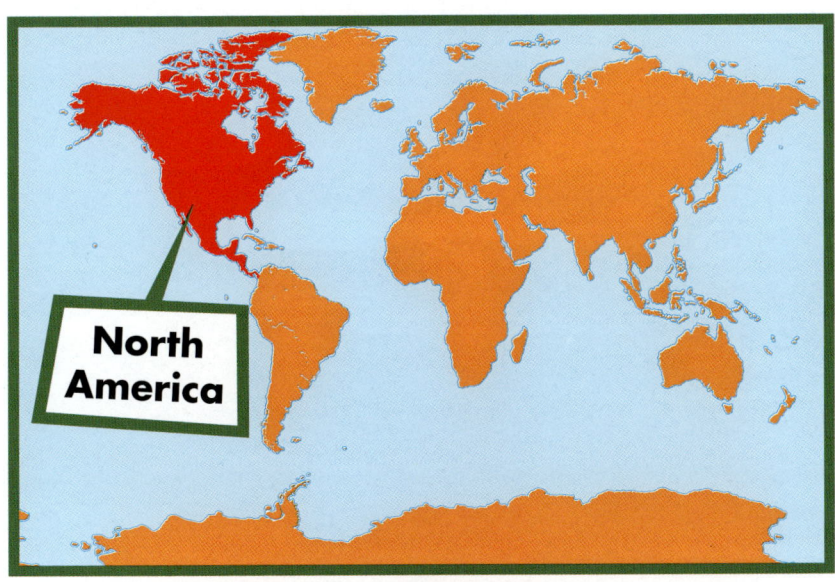

Beavers live in North America, too. They eat bark on trees. They chew trees to build their homes.

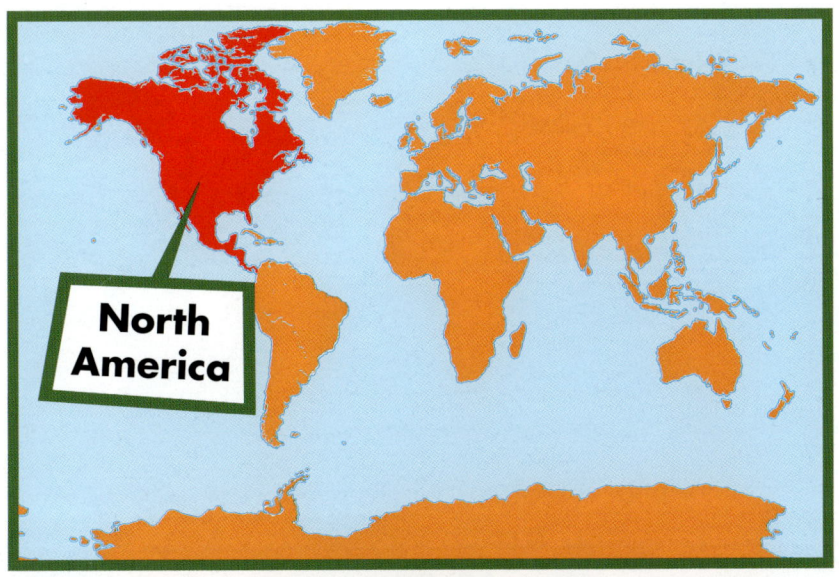

Which wild animals live near your home? What type of food do they eat?

Picture Glossary

beaver
an animal with a wide, flat tail that lives both on land and in water

Cape buffalo
a type of ox with heavy horns found in Africa

rattlesnake
a snake that lives in North America that has a rattle at the end of its tail

spider monkey
a type of monkey that has long skinny arms and legs and a very long tail

tree frog
any one of a type of frog that lives in trees and has round, sticky toes

zebra
an animal from Africa that is like a horse but smaller and has black and white stripes

What Do You Remember?

Look at the world map. Look at the animal pictures. Where does each animal live?

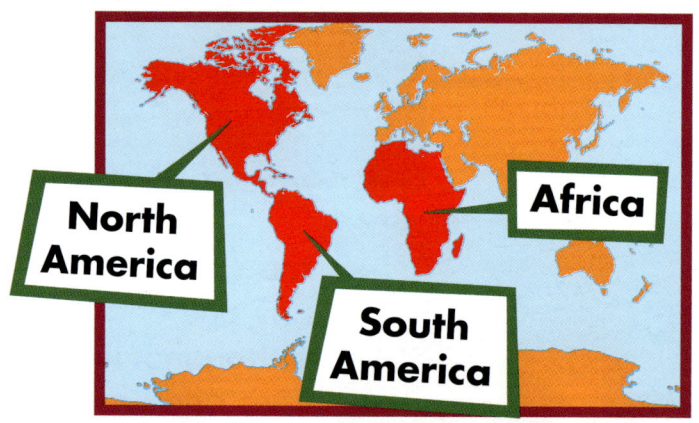

beaver

Cape buffalo

spider monkey

tree frog

rattlesnake

zebra

Ideas for Parents and Teachers

Our Animal World, an Amicus Readers Level 1 series, gives children fascinating facts about animals with lots of reading support. Photo labels and a picture glossary reinforce new vocabulary. The activity page reinforces comprehension and critical thinking. Use the ideas listed below to help children get even more out of their reading experience.

Before Reading

- Talk with children about wild animals and where they live. Ask: What do you know about wild animals?
- Have children look at the cover photo. Ask them if any of them know where tree frogs live in the wild. Explain that they will find the answer in the book.
- Look at the picture glossary. Read and discuss the words.

Read the Book

- Explain that there are three places where the children will get information—the text, the photo, and the map. Invite them to look at the photo first and describe what they see. Explain that the highlighted continent on the map is where the animals live. Read the names of the continents aloud.
- Read the book to the students, or have them read independently.
- Show the children how to refer back to the picture glossary and read the map labels to understand the full meaning.

After Reading

- Have the children retell what they learned. Use the activity on page 22 to help review the text.
- Prompt the child to think more, asking questions such as *What animals live near us? How do animals find food? Why do some animals live in one place and some in other places?*

Index

Africa 7, 9
bark 17
Cape buffalo 9
beavers 17
fruits 11
grasses 7, 9
insects 12
mice 15
North America 15, 17
nuts 11

rabbits 15
rain forest 11
rats 15
rattlesnakes 15
South America 11, 12
spider monkeys 11
spiders 12
tree frogs 12
zebras 7

Web Sites

Animal Videos, Photos, Facts—National Geographic Kids
http://kids.nationalgeographic.com/Animals/

North America: National Zoo
http://nationalzoo.si.edu/Animals/NorthAmerica/ForKids/default.cfm

San Diego Zoo Kids' Territory
http://www.sandiegozoo.org/kids/index.html